Third and Fifth Position STRING BUILDER

FOREWORD

The Third and Fifth Position String Builder is to be used after ⁞ Builder. However, it may also be used as a continuation of any of the st

In this book, the Violin, Viola, Cello and Bass play together. T however, is a complete unit and may be used separately for class or in book, the pupil is carefully taken step by step through the third and fifth p to find each finger, after which simple shifts are introduced with the sar ⁞ ⁞ ⁞ ⁞ by shifts to these positions with different fingers. Each type of shift is presented and developed with interesting melodies.

This book includes the following bowings: the détaché, the martelé, wrist and finger stroke, collé, spiccato and staccato.

The material in this volume is chosen for its musical interest and its technical value. There are a number of duets which are to be played by either two pupils or with the class divided into two groups. There also are a number of melodies in which the class becomes a string ensemble, each instrument playing a different part. A "p" after the number indicates there is a piano part for that melody.

The material in this book is realistically graded so that only a minimum of explanatory material is required. Suggestions for work by Rote are presented throughout the book.

TECHNICAL PROGRESSION

THE THIRD POSITION

THE FIFTH POSITION

© 1963 (Renewed 1991) BELWIN-MILLS PUBLISHING CORP.
All Rights Administered by WARNER BROS. PUBLICATIONS U.S. INC.
All Rights Reserved including Public Performance for Profit

The Third Position (3rd)

Slide the entire hand up the fingerboard (from the elbow joint) until the 1st finger reaches the 3rd finger. As in the 1st position, the thumb is placed opposite the 1st finger or a bit behind it, with a space between the base of the thumb and the neck. In the 3rd position the fingers are placed a bit closer to each other.

"t" means to test the note with the open string. Leave the finger on the string while testing.

Finding the Fingers on the G String

There is a half step between the 3rd and 4th fingers. This is the 3⌢4 finger pattern.

W.B. - means to use the whole bow.

L½ - Lower half of the bow.

Finding the Fingers on the D String

There is a half step between the 3rd and 4th fingers. This is the 3⌢4 finger pattern.

When you test a note, adjust the finger so that it will sound exactly like the open string. By the way, is your Viola in tune? Let us make sure.

Let's Skip A Bit
(in the 3rd Position)

U½ - Use the upper half of the bow.

ROTE PROJECT: In the 3rd position - practice the 3⌢4 finger pattern on the G and D strings. There will be a half step between the 3rd and 4th fingers. Play in various rhythms and bowings.

E.L.1938

© 1963 (Renewed 1991) BELWIN-MILLS PUBLISHING CORP.
All Rights Administered by WARNER BROS. PUBLICATIONS U.S. INC.
All Rights Reserved including Public Performance for Profit

Finding the Fingers on the A and C Strings

On the A string there is a half step between the 2nd and 3rd fingers.

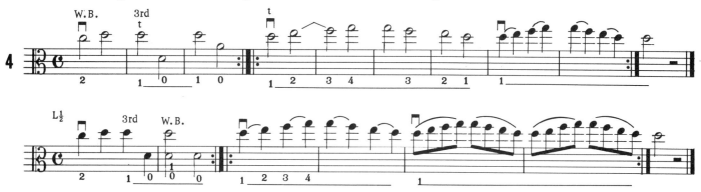

The C String

On the C string all the fingers are a whole step away from each other. The fingers of the left hand should apply more pressure on the strings with the bow hair maintaining a firm grip on the strings.

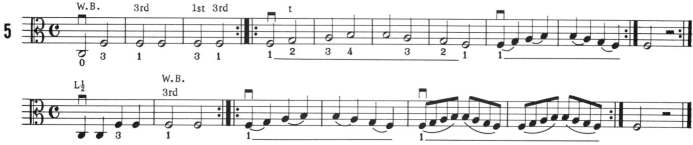

Memorize this rule for the third position in the Key of C:

On the G and D strings there is a half-step between the third and fourth fingers.
On the A string there is a half-step between the second and third fingers.
On the C string there are whole steps between each finger.

The Détaché Bowing

The Détaché is a smooth bowing that may be played in any part of the bow.
Above the middle - only the forearm is to be used from the elbow down. Use the full width of the hair with the stick directly above.

Below the middle - we use the upper arm which moves downward and a bit backward. Use the full width of the hair.

All the Notes in the Third Position

Practice the next 3 lines in 2 ways using the Détaché bowing: (1) $U\frac{1}{2}$ t (2) $L\frac{1}{2}$

These are called Thirds. They are 3 notes apart.

ROTE PROJECT: In the 3rd position - practice the 2 3 finger pattern on the A string. There will be a half step between the 2nd and 3rd fingers. Play in various rhythms and bowings.

E.L.1938

How To Go From One String To Another in the Third Position

In slow string changing we use the arm with a flexible wrist. The bow moves toward the next string to be played and does so in a vertical curve rather than in a straight line. The bow hair is then very close to the next string. This makes it possible to change strings smoothly. When going from one string to another there must not be any break in the tone and the fingers are to remain on the string during the change.

Etude

The first 2 notes of each measure are 4 notes apart and are called FOURTHS.

The last 2 notes of each measure are 3 notes apart and are called THIRDS.

A comma ( ) means a slight pause, usually at the end of a phrase. Leave the bow on the string.

The slanted lines (//) mean to lift the bow from the string.

The "p" after a number indicates that there is a piano part for the melody.

Menuet

Leopold Mozart was the father of the famous Wolfgang Mozart. He was a Violinist and the author of an early Violin method.

The small notes are to be stopped by the fingers but not played

More Melodies From One String To Another in the Third Position

Sonatina (Duet)

Cornelius Gurlitt (1820-1901) was a German organist and composer. This is a movement from one of his piano sonatinas arranged for two Violas.

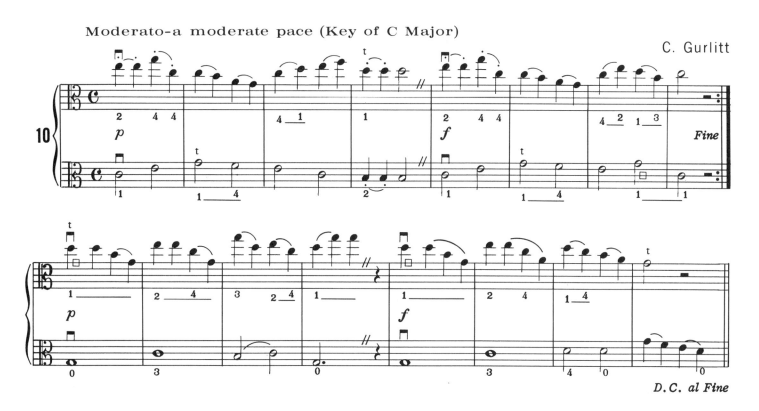

Song of the Harvest (Duet)

Wolfgang Amadeus Mozart (1756-1791) was one of the world's most gifted composers. He started to compose when he was 5 years old.

6

Melodies that go from an Open String to the Third Position

Play each of these a few times very slowly.   Listen carefully to the intonation.

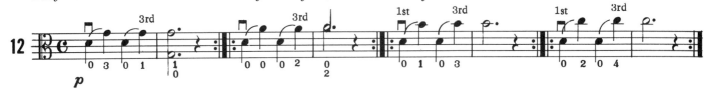

Etude

Moderato (Key of C Major)

C. Hohmann

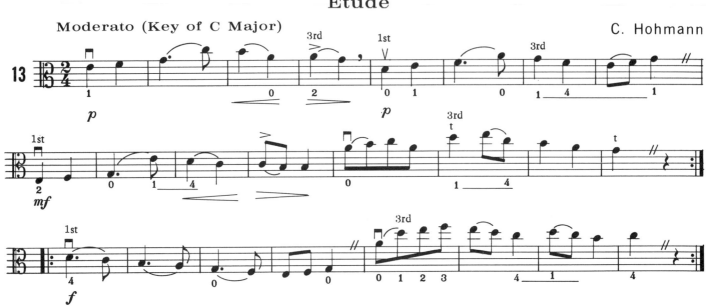

Folk Tune (Ensemble)

This melody is used by Engelbert Humperdinck (1854-1921) in his opera Hansel and Gretel.

From the German

Allegretto (Key of G Major)

ROTE PROJECT: The C Major Scale in two octaves. Start on open C. Play the second octave in the third position, going up to the third position with the first finger on the G string. Descending, go down to the first position with the second finger on the G string. Play each note four, three, and two times, and finally each note once. Practice in various rhythms and bowings.

E.L.1938

Melodies that Shift to the Third Position with the Same Finger

The shift upward is made with the entire hand, the thumb moving with the finger and not lagging behind. On the downward shift, the thumb moves in advance of the finger. During the slide you must lighten the finger pressure on the string and relax the thumb pressure on the neck.

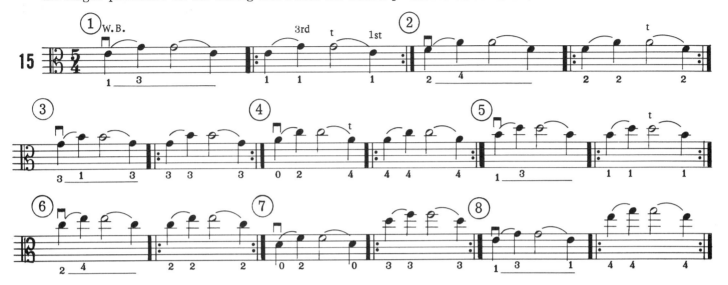

Canzonetta

Allegretto (Key of C Major)   Robert Williams

Sunday Morning

Allegretto (Key of C Major)   W.A. Mozart

E.L.1938

Melodies that Shift with the Same Finger in the Keys of G and D

The White Steeple

Silas J. Vail

Moderato (Key of G Major)

Easter Time

from Lyra Davidica

Allegretto (Key of D Major)

ROTE PROJECT: The G Major Scale in one octave in the 3rd position. Practice in various rhythms and bowings. Refer to the C Major Scale on Page 6.

Melodies that Shift By Scale Line to the Third Position

1. When we shift to a note in the third position by scale line we slide with the finger THAT WE ARE GOING TO.
   The finger that we are going to actually displaces the finger that is on the string.

2. When we shift from the third position by scale line to a note in the first position, we slide with the finger THAT IS ON THE STRING.

   The small notes are not to be played. They serve as a guide to the finger that is sliding. The pitch of the small note is approximate.

The Carnival of Venice with a Variation

Niccolo Paganini (1782-1840) was perhaps the first Violin virtuoso. His compositions for the Violin are widely used.

Allegretto (Key of G Major)

N. Paganini

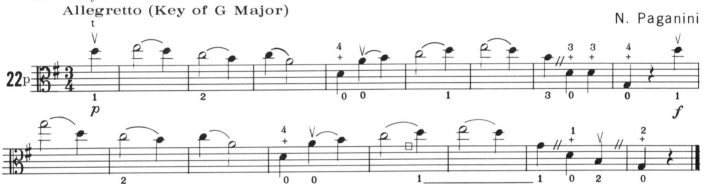

The Wrist and Finger Bowing

For this bowing use only the wrist and fingers. Start with all fingers curved and the middle joint of the thumb bent outward. Draw the bow down with the wrist about 2 inches, straightening the fingers at the same time. Now draw the bow up about 2 inches curving the fingers. Practice this stroke a few minutes each day.

Variation

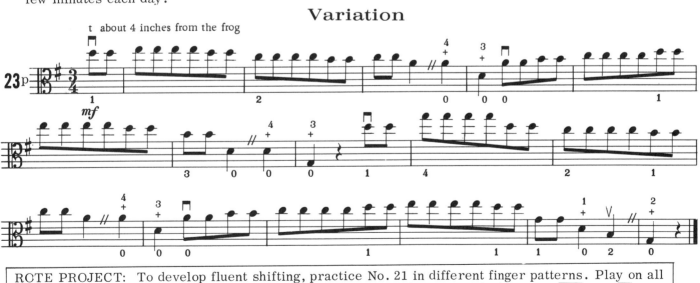

ROTE PROJECT: To develop fluent shifting, practice No. 21 in different finger patterns. Play on all strings in various rhythms and tempi. For example:

10

Melodies that Shift By Scale Line in the Keys of F and G Minor
Gavotte (Duet with Piano)

George F. Handel (1685-1759) was born in the same year as Bach but died 9 years later. A Gavotte is an old dance in 4/4 time usually beginning on the up beat of the measure.

G.F. Handel

Allegretto (Key of F Major)

Greensleeves

Andantino-a bit faster than Andante
(Key of G minor) t

Traditional English Melody

ROTE PROJECT: The F Major Scale in one octave in the 3rd position. Practice in various rhythms and bowings.

E.L.1938

Melodies that Shift to the Third Position with Different Fingers

When ascending, the finger that is on the string slides up until it reaches the third position. When you reach the third position, the finger that you are going to, will strike the string.

When descending, the finger that is on the string slides until it reaches the first position. Then the finger that you are going to will strike the string.

Memorize this basic rule: when we shift to a different finger, the slide is performed with the finger that is on the string.

Practice the following shifts slowly so that the slide between the first and third positions is audible.

Dear Katherine

Allegretto (Key of F Major)

German Folk Song

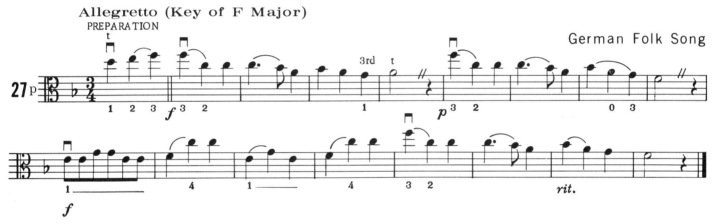

More Shifting with Different Fingers

A Stately Dance

Johann S. Bach was born in Germany in 1685 and died in 1750. He was one of the great organists of his time. His fame as a composer did not start until nearly 100 years after his death, when his works were revived by Felix Mendelssohn.

Moderato (Key of G minor)

J.S. Bach

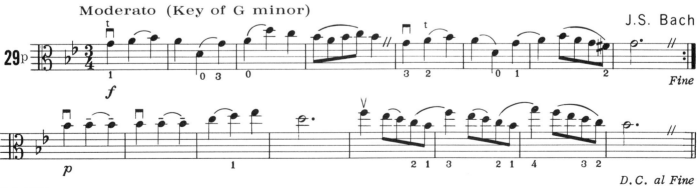

More Melodies that Shift with Different Fingers

Abide With Me

Moderato (Key of B♭ Major) — William H. Monk

How to Shift When There Is No Slur

When we shift and change bows at the same time. we slide upward with the finger that we are going to. We slide downward with the finger that is on the string. Do not permit the slide to be heard.

on D

The Shepherdess

Andante-a moderately slow movement (Key of A minor) — 17th Century Air

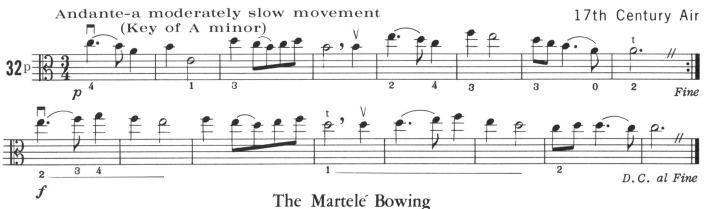

Fine

D.C. al Fine

The Martelé Bowing

This stroke starts with a sharp accent and ends with a clean stop. At the start of the stroke, press the bow into the string. Draw the bow quickly and release this pressure at the same time.

Play this piece in 3 ways: (1) W.B. (2) U$\frac{1}{2}$ (3) L$\frac{1}{2}$

In Praise (Ensemble)

Moderato (Key of D Major) — Alexander Reinagle

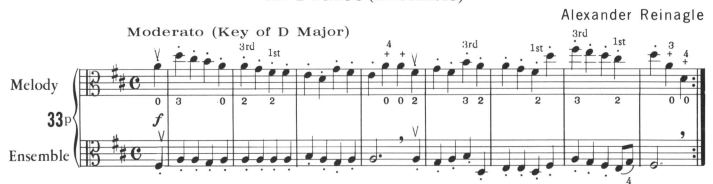

ROTE PROJECT: Two octave scales in the Keys of C, G and D in unison with the Violins. Violas alone in the Keys of E♭ and F. Start each scale in the 1st position. Shift to the 3rd position on the D string with the 1st finger. Descending, shift to the 1st position on the D string with the 2nd finger. Try a minor scale.

E.L.1938

Melodies that Will Teach Us How to Play Harmonics

One full step above the 4th finger in the 3rd position on each string, we will find a harmonic which is an octave higher than the open string. The hand remains in the 3rd position while the 4th finger flattens out and stretches to the harmonic. A clear harmonic will be produced if the string is lightly touched in the right spot. The other fingers are to be lifted from the string.

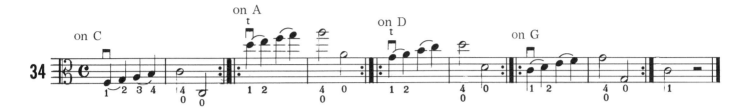

Passepied

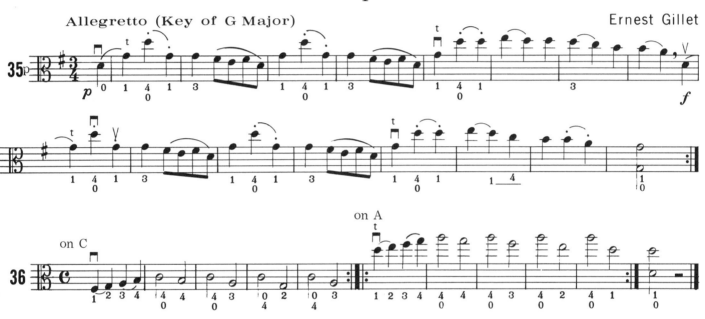

Ernest Gillet

Theme

Franz Schubert (1797-1828) composed a great deal in his short life. This is a theme from his famous Unfinished Symphony.

Franz Schubert

The Fifth Position—How To Find the First Finger

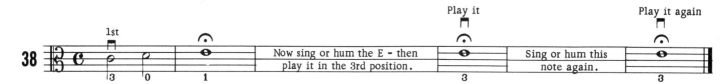

Now bring the left thumb around under the neck so that it is practically at right angles. The thumb should contact the base of the neck between the middle joint and the tip of the thumb. The lower arm must turn inward. We now draw the bow closer to the bridge.

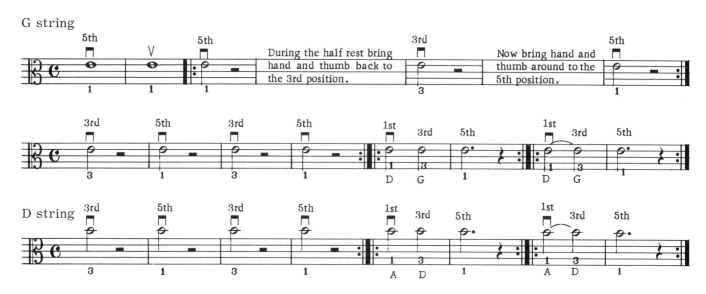

On the A string, the 1st finger in the 5th position is placed a bit lower than the 1st finger on the C, D and A strings.

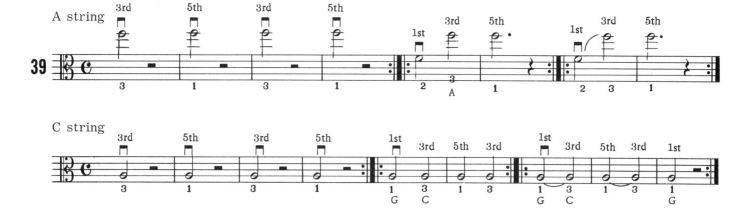

A Technical Stunt
The Rhythm Band

Moderato (Key of C Major).

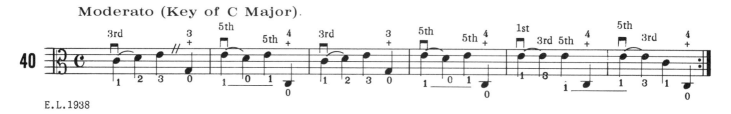

E.L.1938

Finding the Second Finger in the Fifth Position

On the G and D strings, the 2nd finger is a half step from the 1st finger.

In the 5th position the fingers are placed closer to each other than in the lower positions.

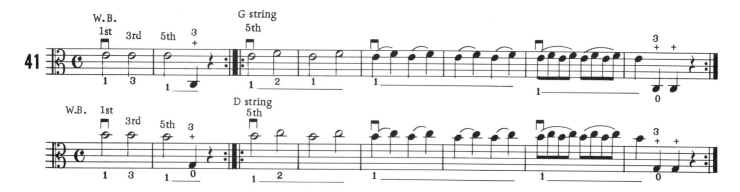

On the A and C strings, the 2nd finger is a whole step from the 1st finger.

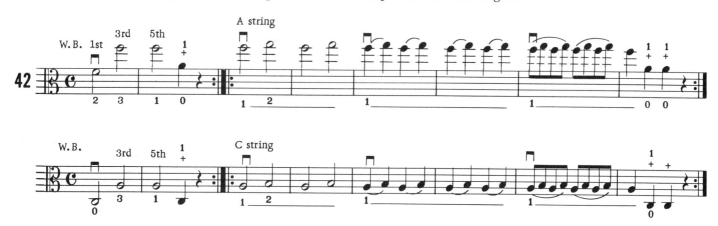

The First on D and the First on A (in the 5th Position)— What is the Difference?

In the 9th measure, use the staccato bowing, which is a series of martelé notes in the same bow. Play them above the middle of the bow using the full width of the hair.

Etude

E.L.1938

Finding the Third and Fourth Fingers in the Fifth Position

On the G and D strings. the 3rd finger is a whole step from the 2nd finger, and the 4th finger is a whole step from the 3rd finger.

Use the whole bow throughout this page.

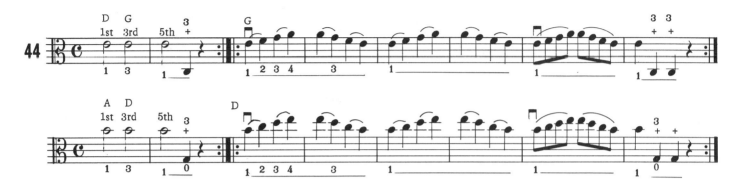

On the A string all the fingers are a whole step apart in the 5th position.

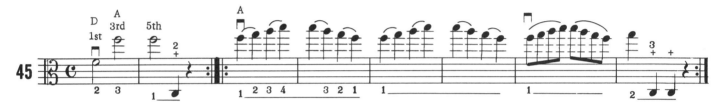

On the C string (in the 5th position) the 3rd finger C is a half step from the 2nd finger B. The 4th finger D is a whole step from the 3rd finger C.

From One String To Another in the Fifth Position

Try to keep the fingers down when going from one string to another. Notice the treble clef.

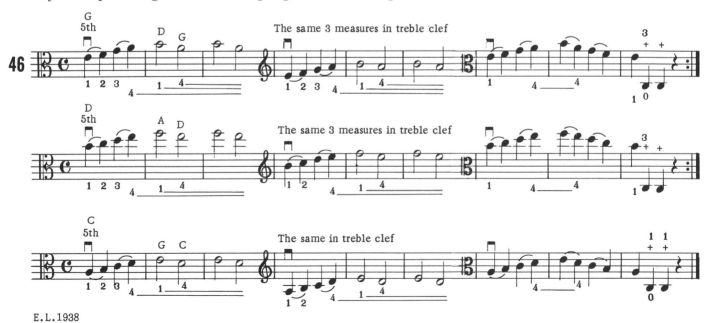

E.L.1938

Melodies That Go From One String To Another in the Fifth Position
A Melodious Etude

Moderato (Key of C Major)

Ch. De Beriot

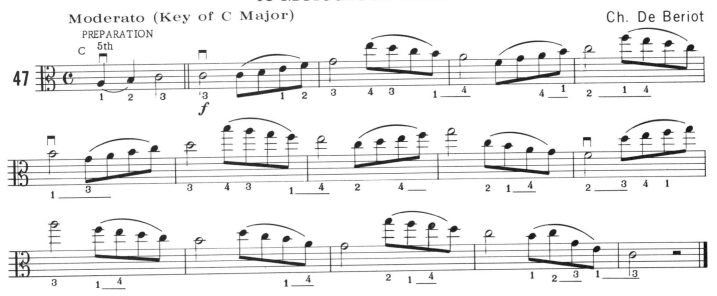

Bourée (Duet)

A Bourrée is a lively dance of French or Spanish origin beginning with an up-beat. It is usually in 4/4 or 2/4 time.

Allegretto (Key of C Major)

J.S. Bach

ROTE PROJECT: In the 5th position - practice the 1̂ 2 finger pattern on the G and D strings. There will be a half step between the 1st and 2nd fingers. Play in various rhythms and bowings.

More Melodies From One String To Another in the Fifth Position

Etude in Scales

Moderato (Key of C Major)

Ch. De Beriot

Practice in 2 ways: (1) above the middle (A.M.) (2) below the middle (B.M.)

The Grand Martelé

For the Grand Martelé, we use the entire bow. The martelé attack at the tip must be just as firm and sharp as the attack at the frog. Do not allow the bow to slide down on the fingerboard as you approach the tip.

The Gypsy King

Moderato (Key of C Major)

Old Hungarian Air

ROTE PROJECT: In the 5th position - the whole tone finger pattern starting on F on the A string. There will be a whole step between each note. Practice in various rhythms and bowings.

E.L.1938

Melodious Etudes in the Fifth Position in the Keys of G and F

The Dutch Door

Moderato (Key of G Major)

F. Wohlfahrt

The Gossip

Use the Détaché bowing. Practice in 2 ways: (1) U 1/3 (2) L 1/3.

Moderato (Key of F Major)

F. Wohlfahrt

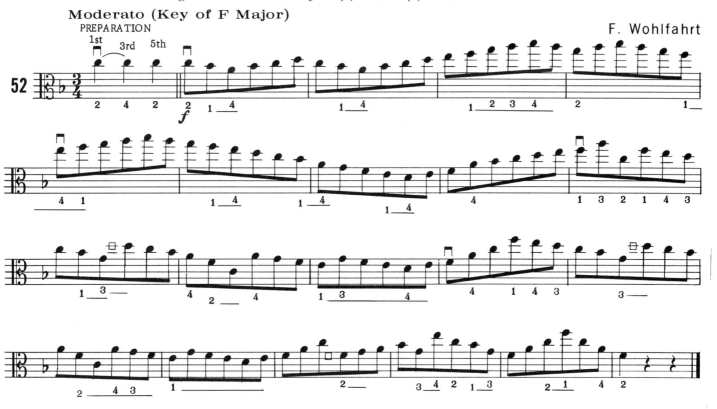

ROTE PROJECT: In the 5th position - practice the 2 3 finger pattern on the C string. There will be a half step betwen the 2nd and 3rd fingers. Play in various rhythms and bowings.

E.L.1938

From the Third Position We Shift to the Fifth Position with the Same Finger

Concentrate on your left thumb and lighten the finger pressure on the string as you shift.

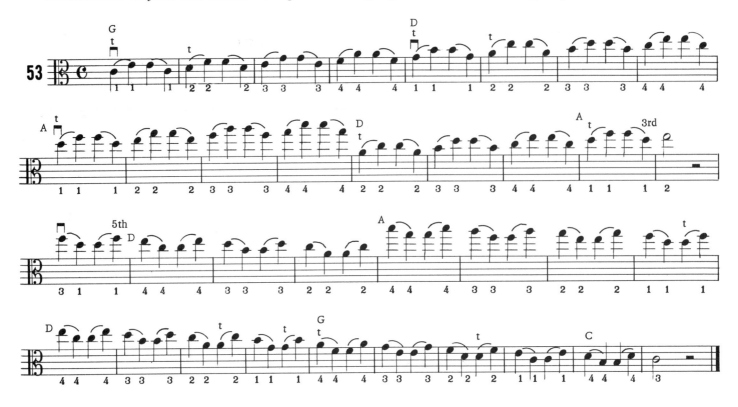

From the Third Position We Shift to the Fifth Position with Different Fingers

I Love Thee

Edvard Grieg (1843-1907) is Norway's best loved omposer. He composed many songs as well as the famous "Peer Gynt Suite".

Edvard Grieg

Andante (Key of C Major)

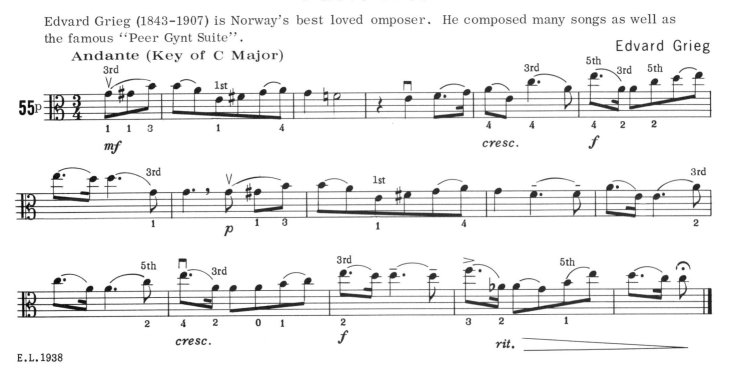

E.L.1938

We Shift to the Fifth Position with the Same Finger in Various Keys

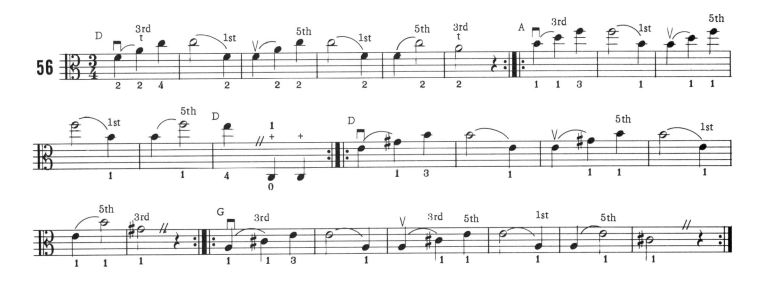

When the last note in a slur is marked with a dot it is held a bit less than its value. Do not accent this note, but leave a slight pause after the note has been played. The comma (❜) indicates a slight pause with the bow remaining on the string. The slanted lines (//) mean that the bow is to be lifted from the string.

Fantasy

Georg P. Telemann (1681-1767) lived at the same time as Bach. He wrote many operas, oratorios and instrumental works.

G. Telemann

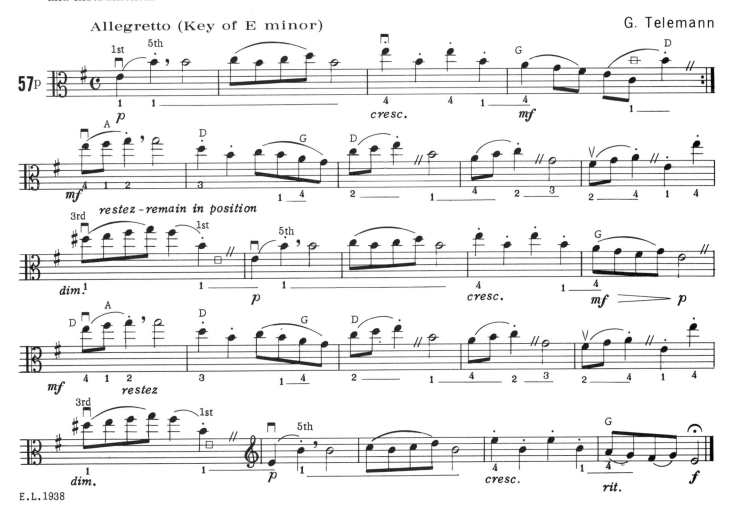

How to Shift from the Third Position to the Fifth Position By Scale Line

1. When we shift from the third position by scale line to a note in the fifth position, we slide with the finger THAT WE ARE GOING TO.

   Be sure to bring the thumb well around and under to the base of the neck as you go to the fifth position.

2. When we shift from the fifth position by scale line to a note in the third position, we slide with the finger THAT IS ON THE STRING.

   The small notes are not to be played. They serve as a guide to the finger that is sliding.

The Collé Bowing

This is a wrist and finger stroke which starts with the bow on the string. Place the bow firmly on the string at the frog with all the fingers curved. Press the bow firmly into the string by pinching the bow. Release the pressure on the bow, moving it slightly down-bow with the bow leaving the string. As you release the pinch, the fingers straighten out. When playing the collé up-bow, start about two inches from the frog, with the fingers straight. As you release the pinch and go up-bow, the fingers become curved.

Practice this scale in two ways: (1) all down-bows   (2) all up-bows.

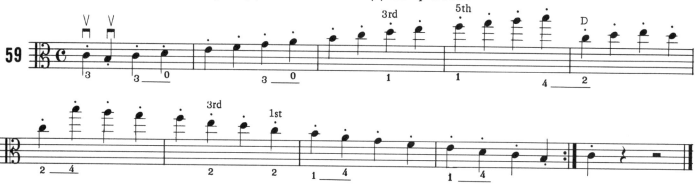

The Gypsy King

Allegretto (Key of C Major)

Old Hungarian Air

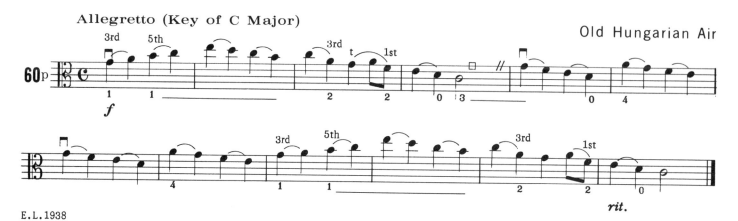

Melodies that Shift to the Fifth Position By Scale Line in Various Keys

Practice in 2 ways: (1) $U\frac{1}{2}$ (2) $L\frac{1}{2}$

Hallelujah (Duet)

Moderato (Key of F Major)   Round in Two Parts

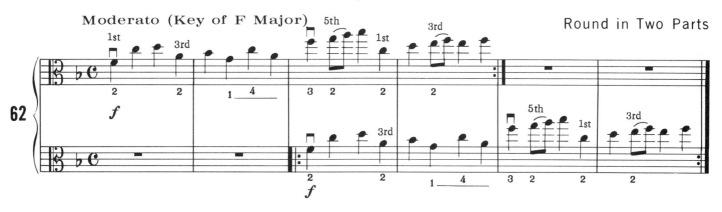

Theme from Concerto Grosso in D

Largo-very slow (Key of D Major)   A. Corelli

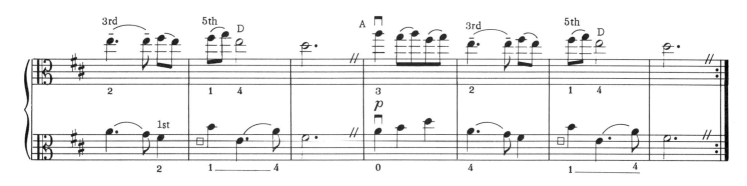

ROTE PROJECT: To develop fluent shifting, practice No. 58 in different finger patterns. Play on all strings in various rhythms and tempi. For example:

Try playing in artificial harmonics to develop the "1st to the 4th" finger relationship.

E.L.1938

24

Melodies in the First, Third, and Fifth Positions

A Graceful Dance (Ensemble)

Allegretto (Key of D Major)

H. Purcell

An English Dance

Old Dance Tune

Allegretto (Key of F Major)

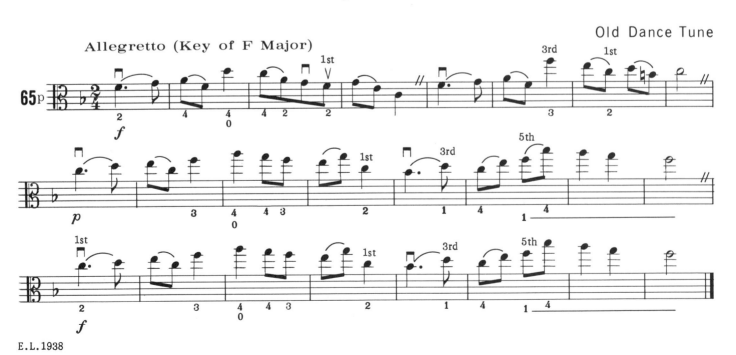

E.L.1938

From the First Position We Shift to the Fifth Position with Different Fingers

Review the text on Page 11. On this page when we shift from the 1st position to the 5th position, we follow this basic rule: Slide with the finger that is on the string.

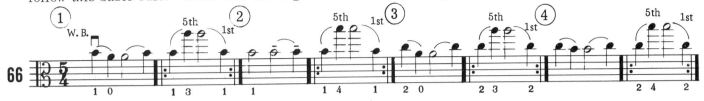

Andante

This is a theme from the slow movement of one of the great Violin concertos.

More Shifting to the Fifth Position

Humoresque

More Melodies that Shift to the Fifth Position with Different Fingers

Juanita

Andantino (Key of G Major)

Spanish Melody

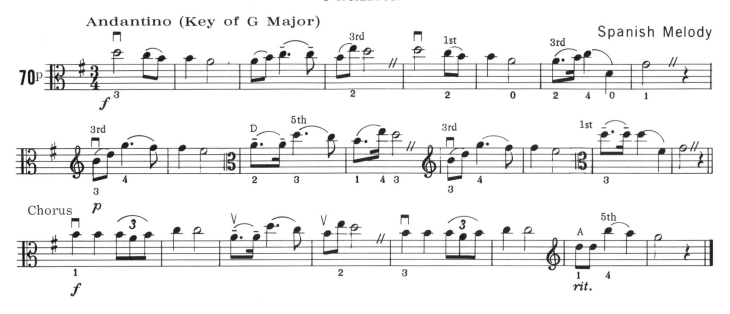

Chorus

For Gretchen (Duet)

Moderato (Key of G Major)

German Song

Interesting Melodies Using the Martelé and Staccato Bowings

A Polyphonic Dance (Duet)

Allegretto (Key of A minor)

G. Telemann

Minuet from "Don Giovanni"

Moderato (Key of F Major)

W.A. Mozart

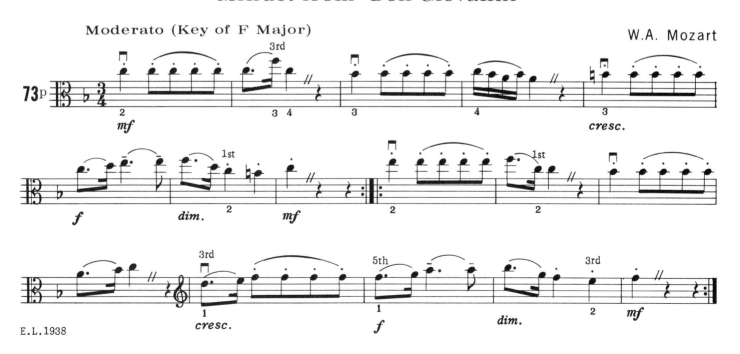

Playing One Octave Scales on a Single String—The Whole Tone Scale

Major Scales

Play the next 5 lines on the G string.   Use the upper half of the bow.

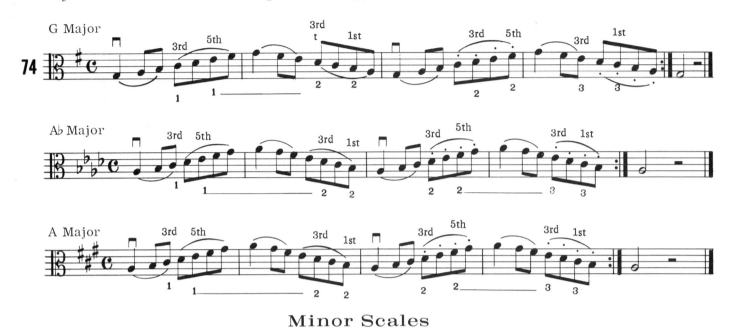

Minor Scales

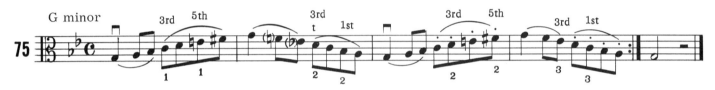

A New Experience in Sound

The Whole Tone Scale

In this scale the notes are a whole step apart.   There are no half steps.
✗- means a double sharp.   The pitch is raised two half steps.

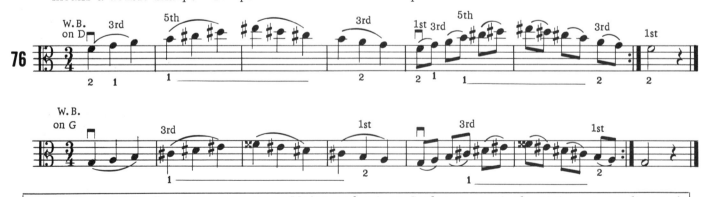

ROTE PROJECT: Practice one octave Major and minor Scales on a single string, ascending and descending with the fingering used in the 1st two measures of Nos. 74 and 75. Play on all strings in various rhythms and bowings.

E.L.1938

Arpeggios in the First, Third, and Fifth Positions

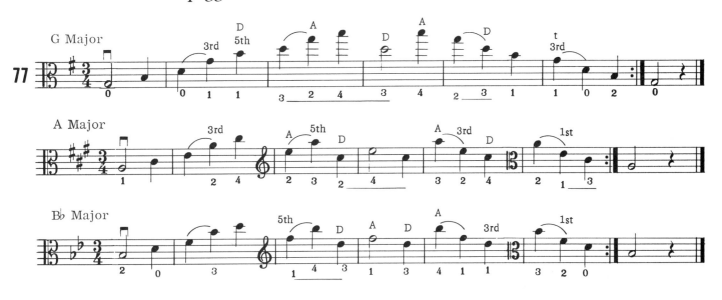

An Arpeggio Etude

C. De Beriot

Moderato (Key of F Major)

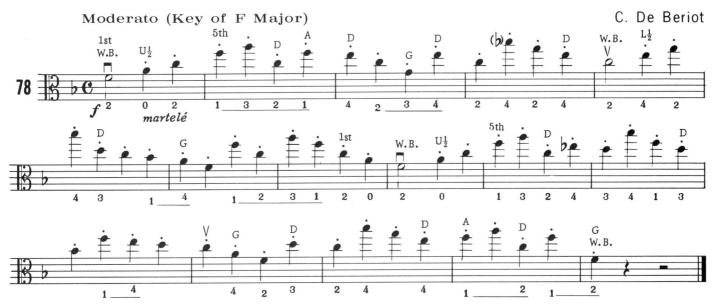

A King Is Crowned

Use the wrist and finger bowing on the 16th notes and the martelé bowing on the 8th notes marked with dots.

F. Wohlfahrt

Moderato (Key of G Major)

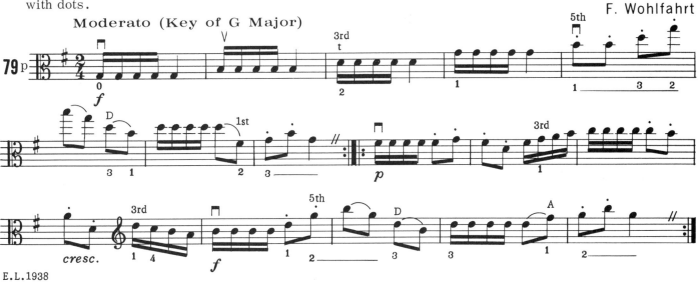

E.L.1938

Lively Melodies Using the Spiccato Bowing
Polonaise

A Polonaise is a stately Polish dance in 3/4 time.

Use the spiccato bowing on all the 8th notes marked with dots and the martelé bowing on the quarter
notes marked with dots.

Allegretto (Key of C Major)

Leopold Mozart's Notebook

Quick Air

Vivace-lively (Key of G minor)

Henry Purcell

ROTE PROJECT: In the 5th position - practice one octave Major Scales in the Keys of C, F, B♭, G
and D. End each scale on one note above the octave before descending. Use the whole bow détaché
and martelé strokes in separate bows, as well as the slow spiccato stroke, playing each note 4, 3,
and 2 times.

Two Minuets in the First, Third, and Fifth Positions

Minuet

Allegretto (Key of C Major)

18th Century Dance

Minuet (Duet)

Use the martelé on the quarter notes and the spiccato on the 8th notes marked with dots.

Allegretto (Key of G Major)

G.F. Handel

E.L.1938

Samuel Applebaum

has contributed much in the field of study material for the strings. In the gathering of material for his work, he has held innumerable conferences and worked countless hours with leading string specialists of the world.

STRINGS ARE AT THEIR BEST
WITH APPLEBAUM BOOKS

Get Acquainted With His

—BELWIN—
STRING BUILDER

A String Class Method
(for class or individual instruction)
IN THREE VOLUMES

SCALES FOR STRINGS

IN TWO VOLUMES

BUILDING TECHNIQUE WITH
BEAUTIFUL MUSIC

IN TWO VOLUMES